A STRESS RELIEF COLORING BOOK

DREAM CATCHER

VOL.1

COLOR TEST PAGE

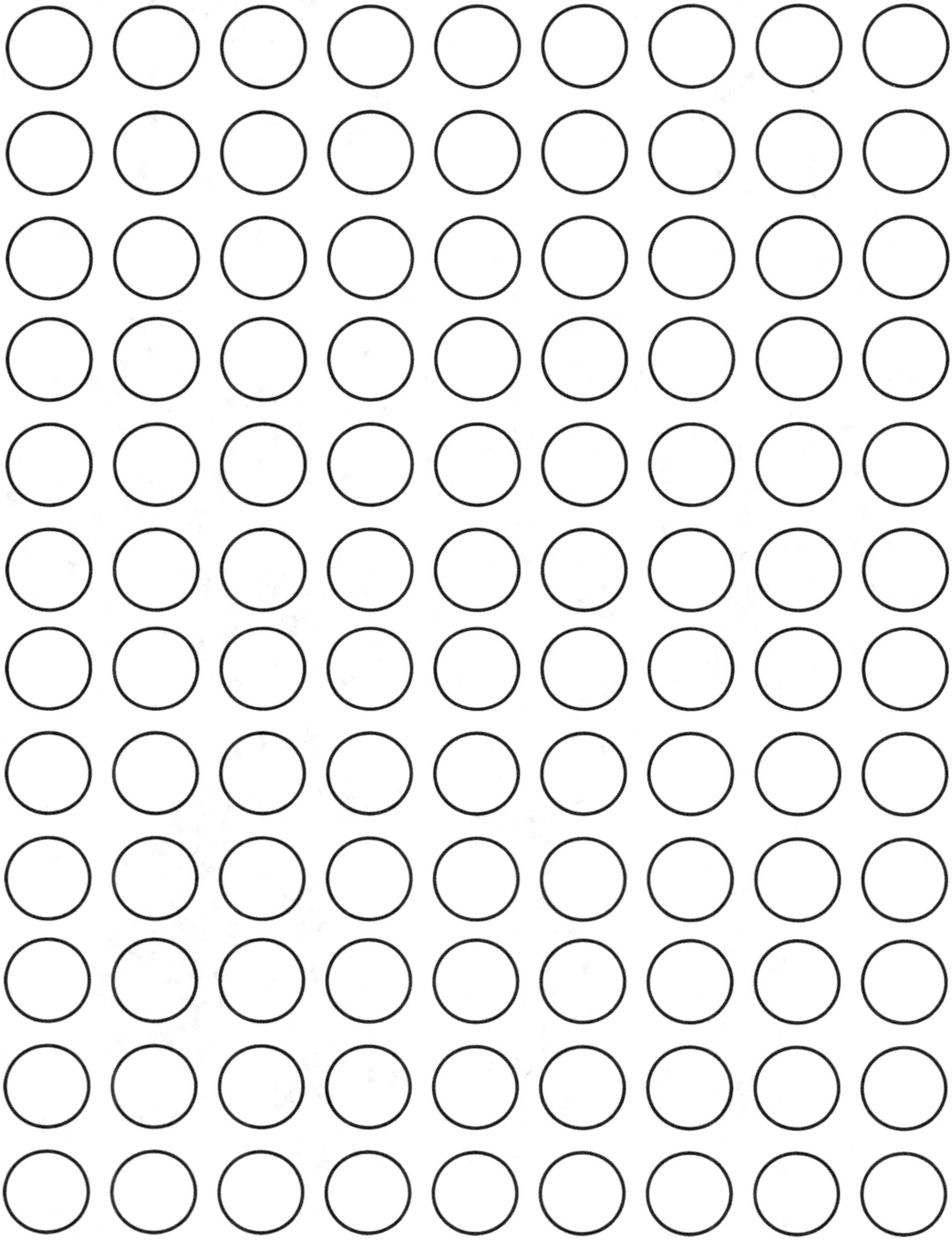

COLOR TEST PAGE

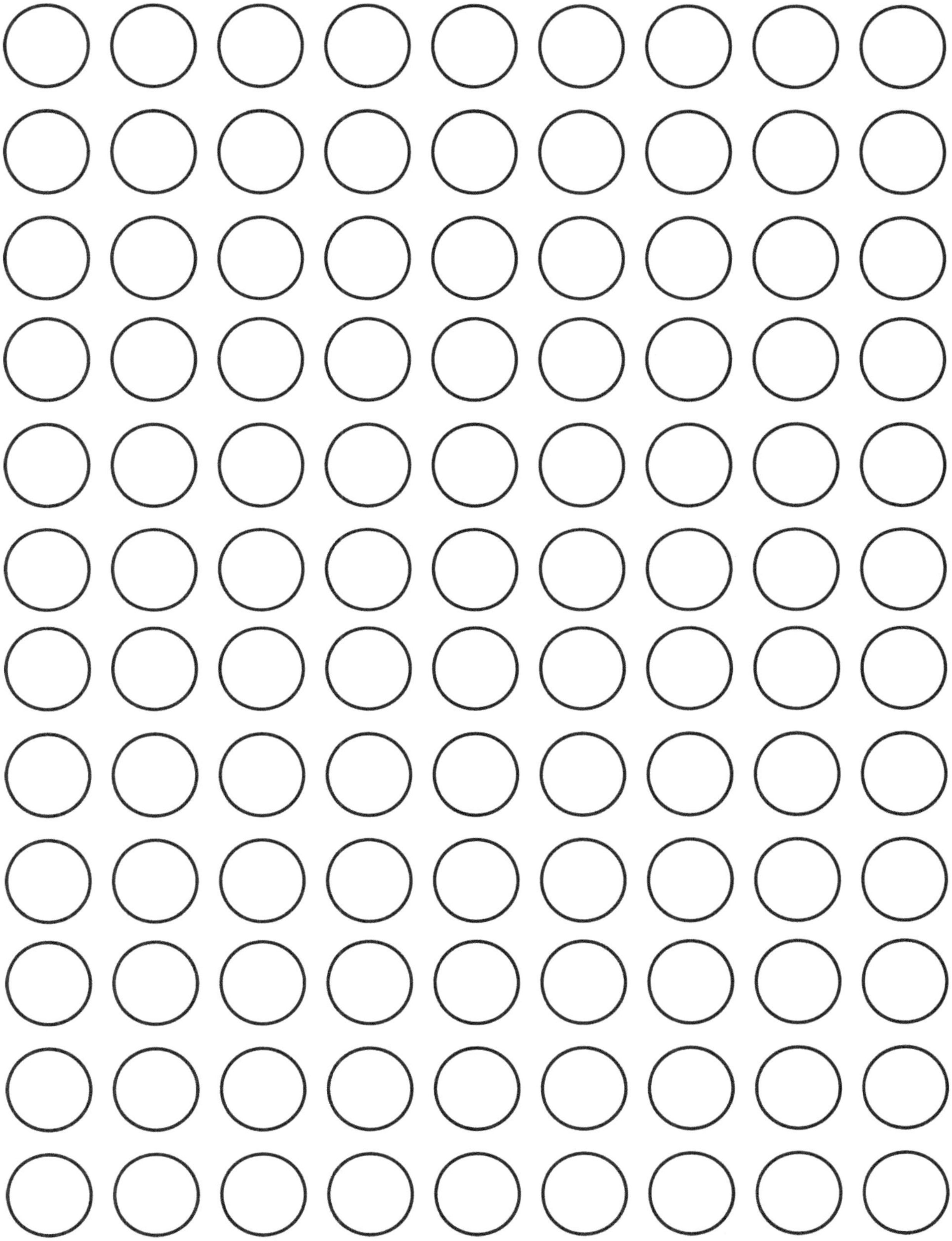

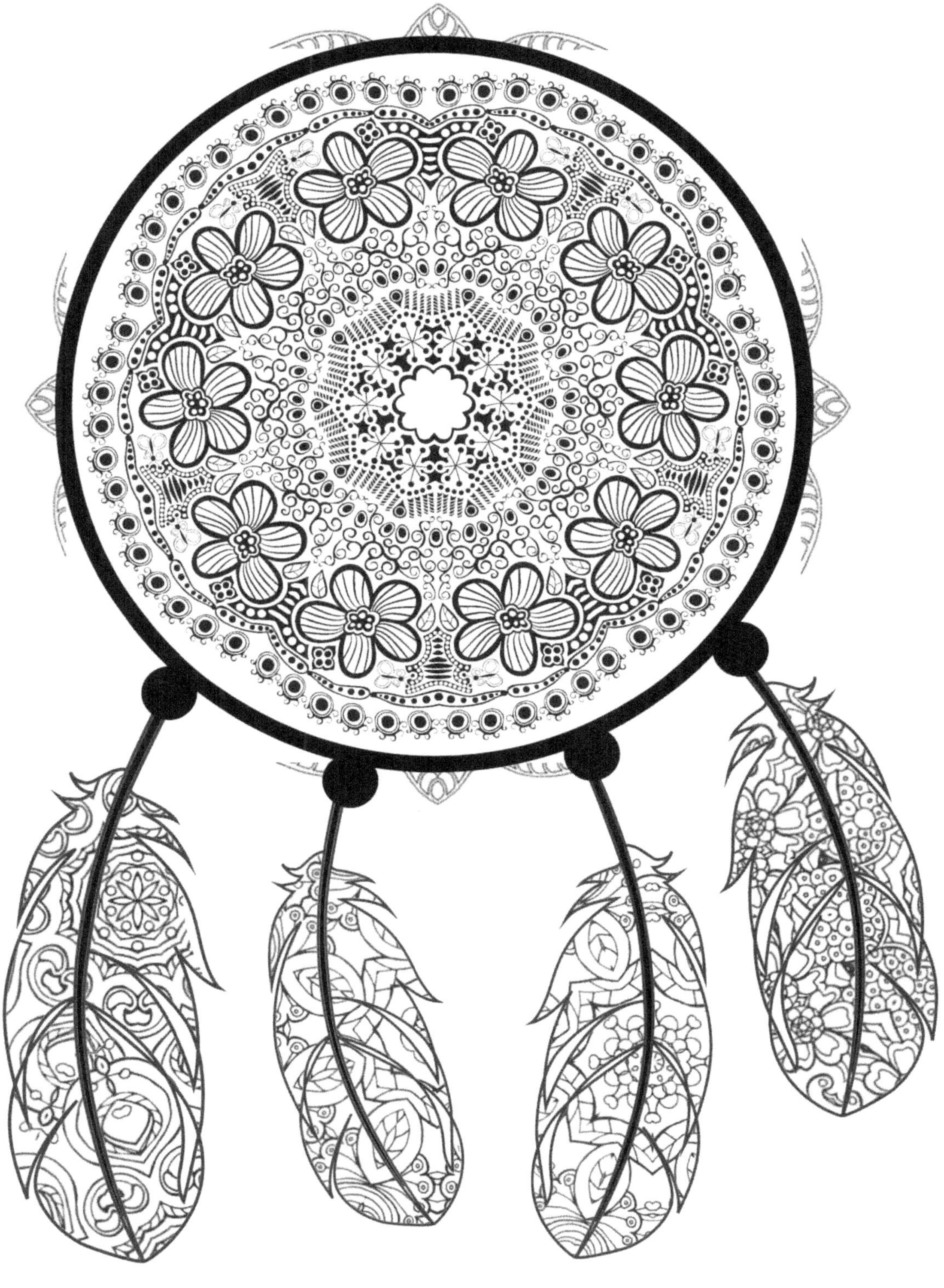

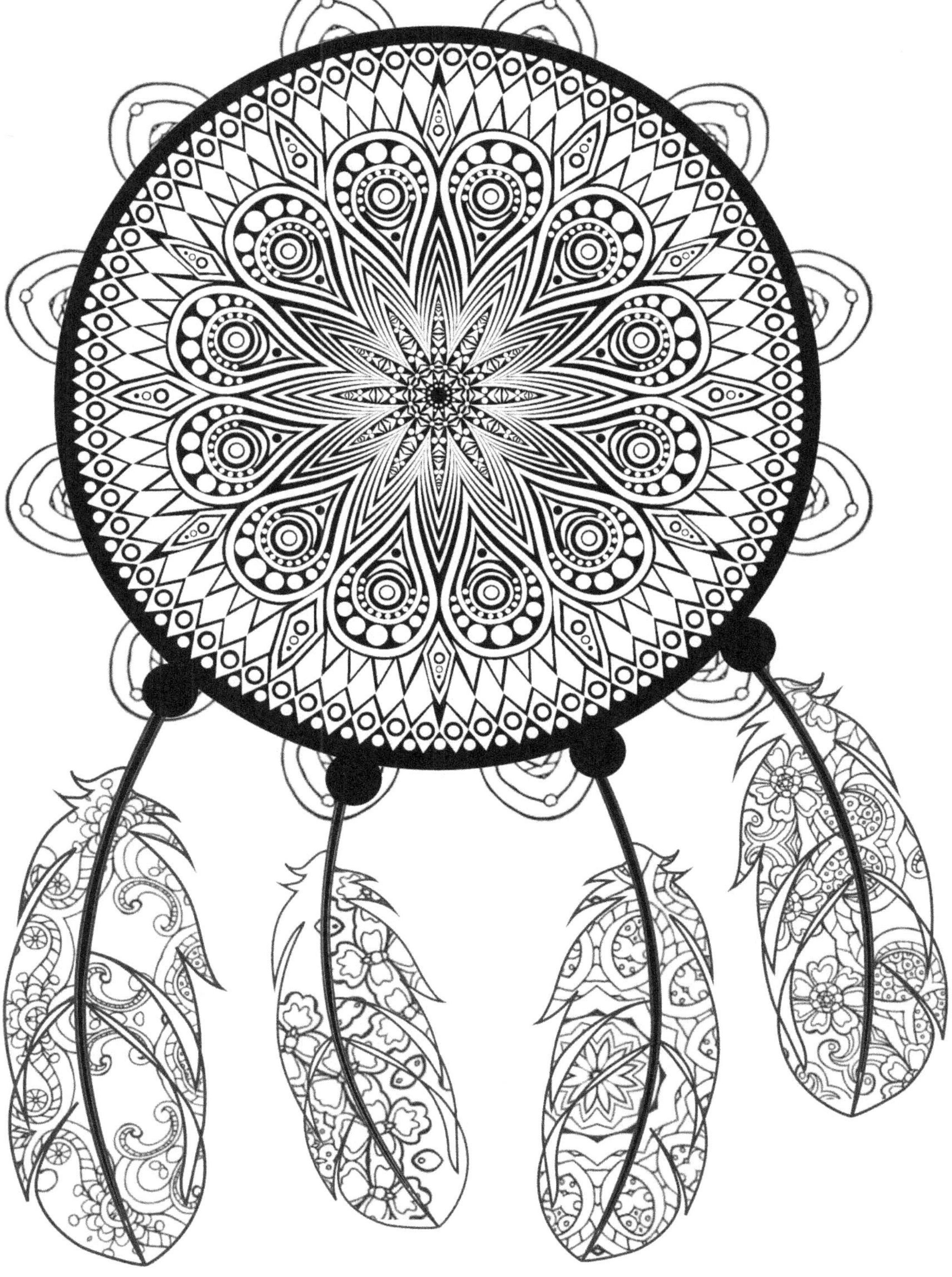

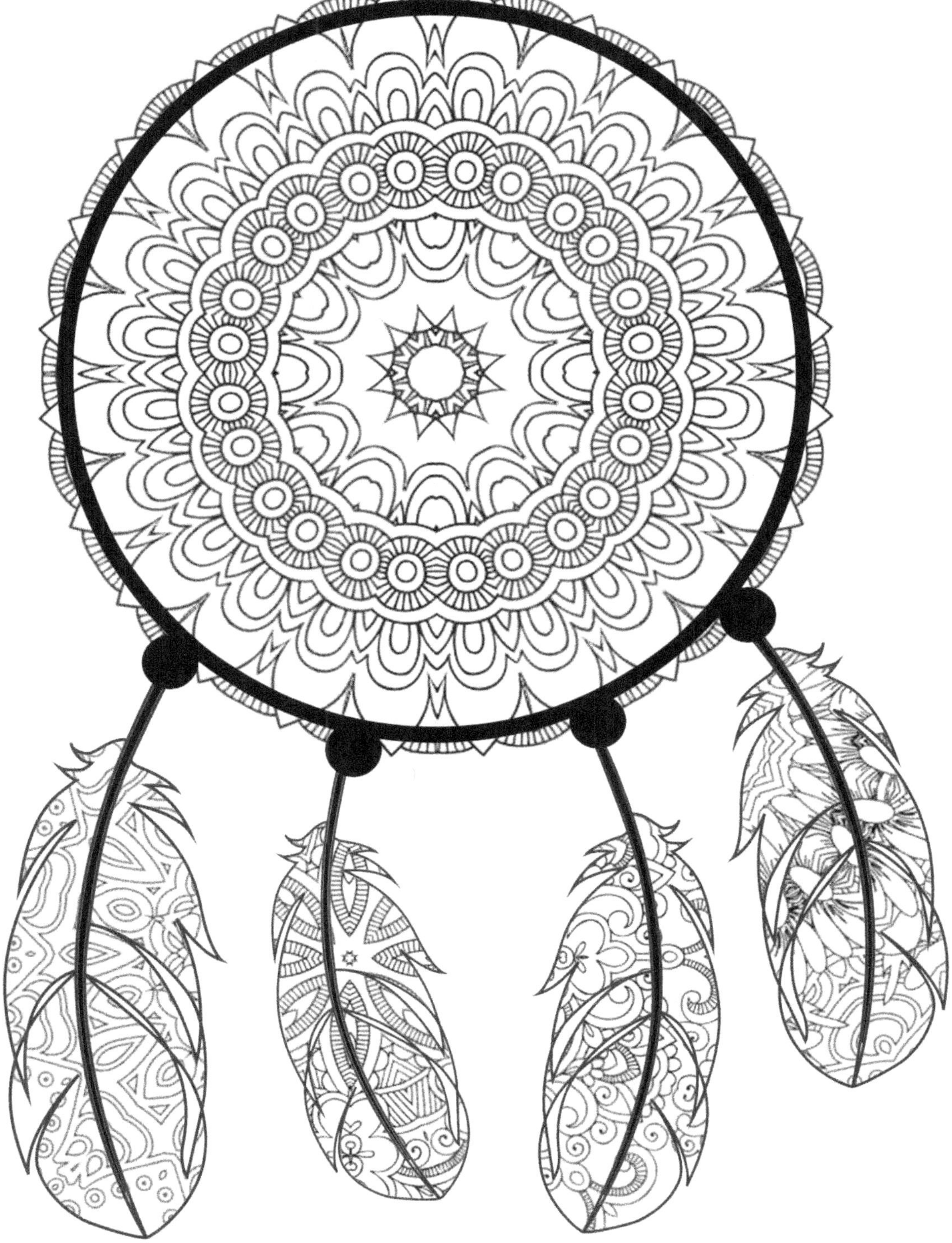

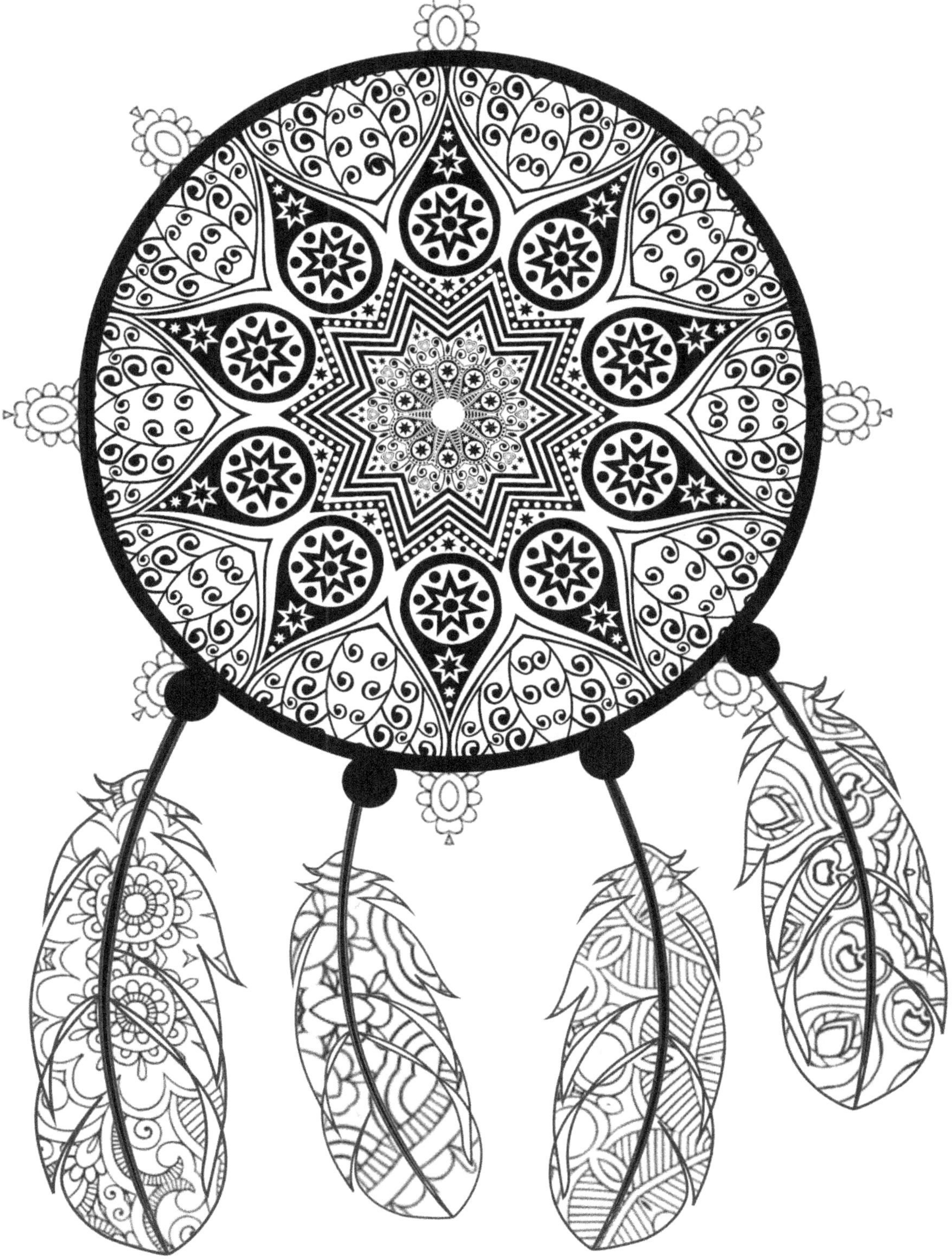

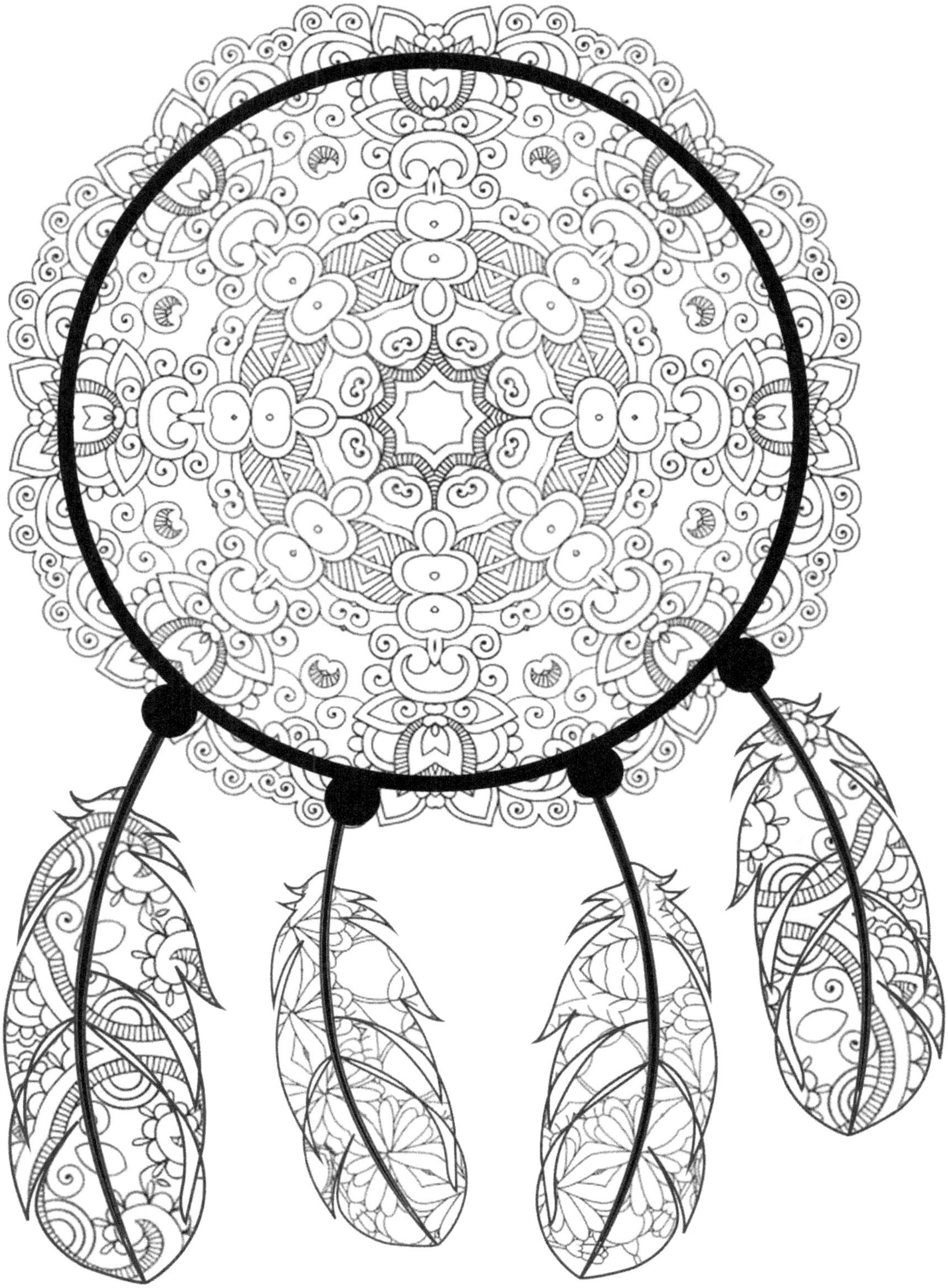

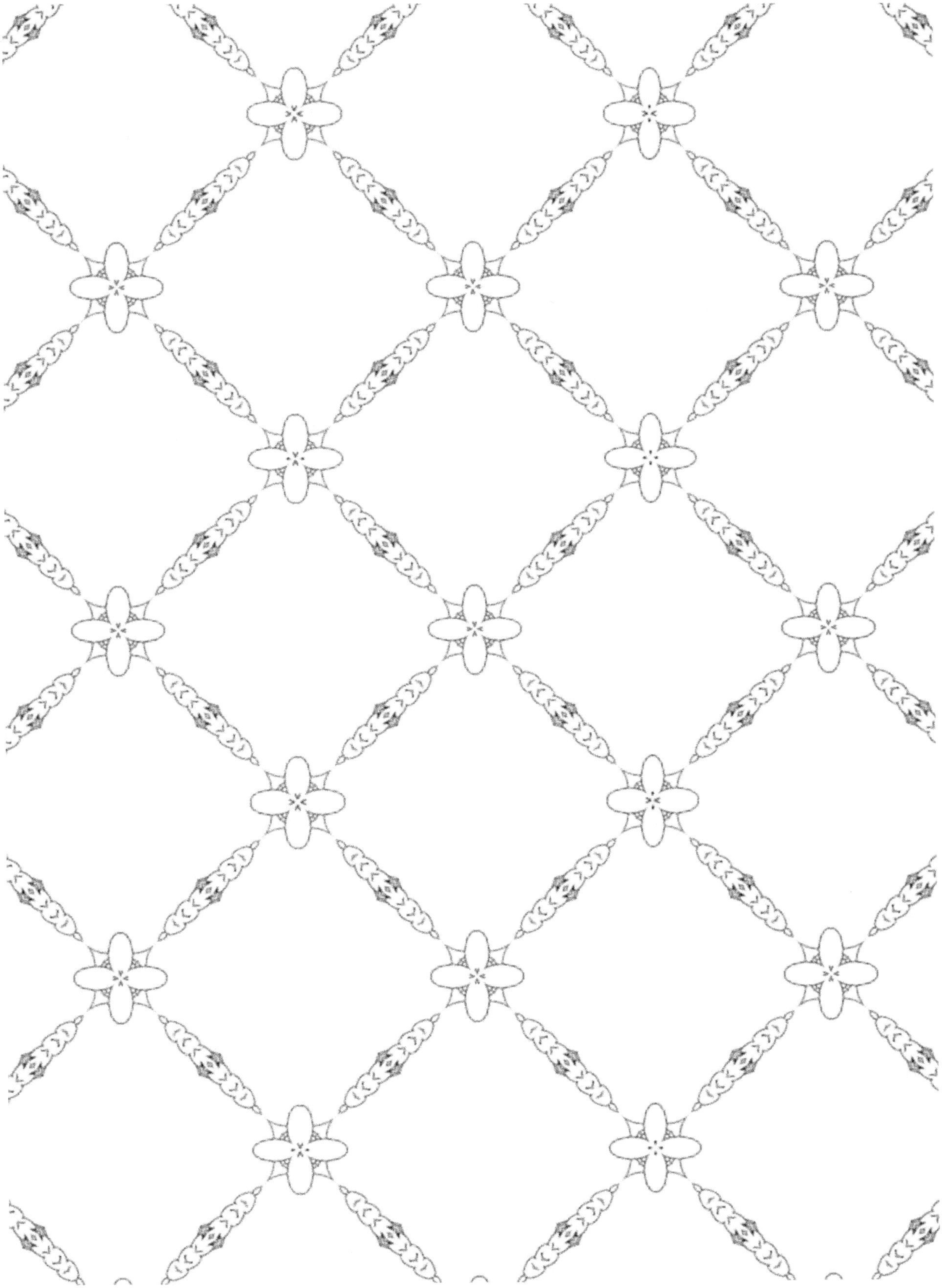

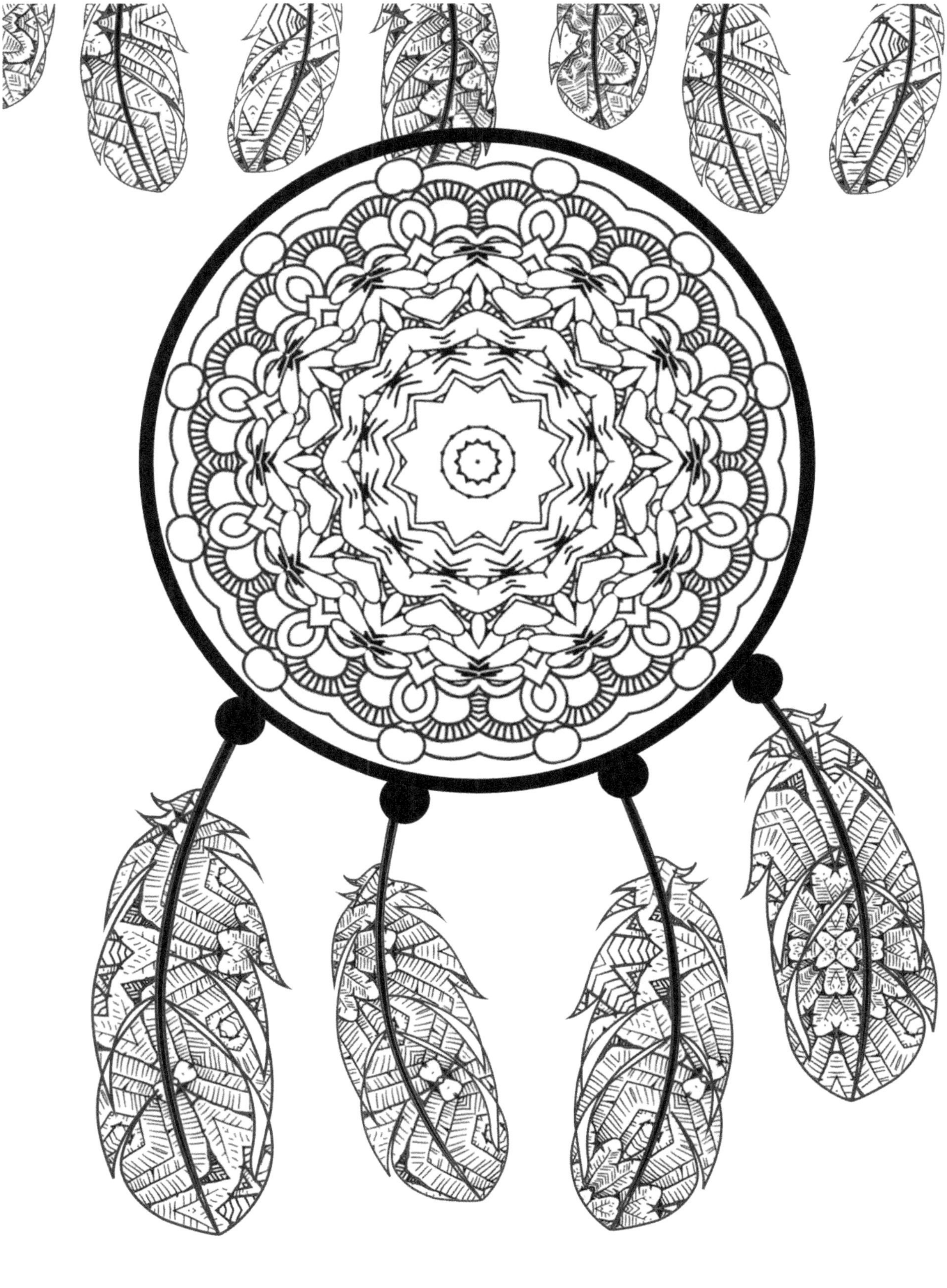

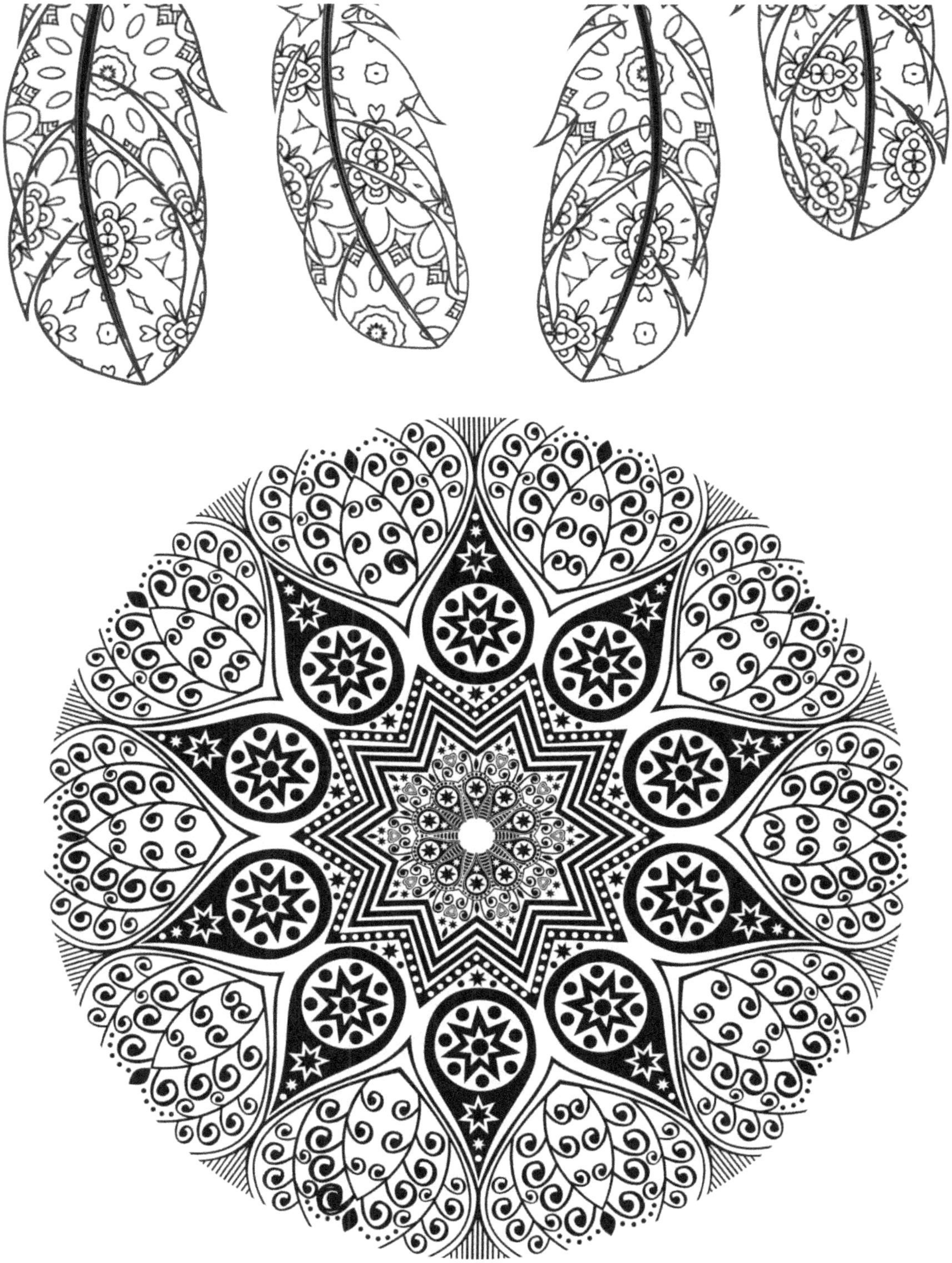

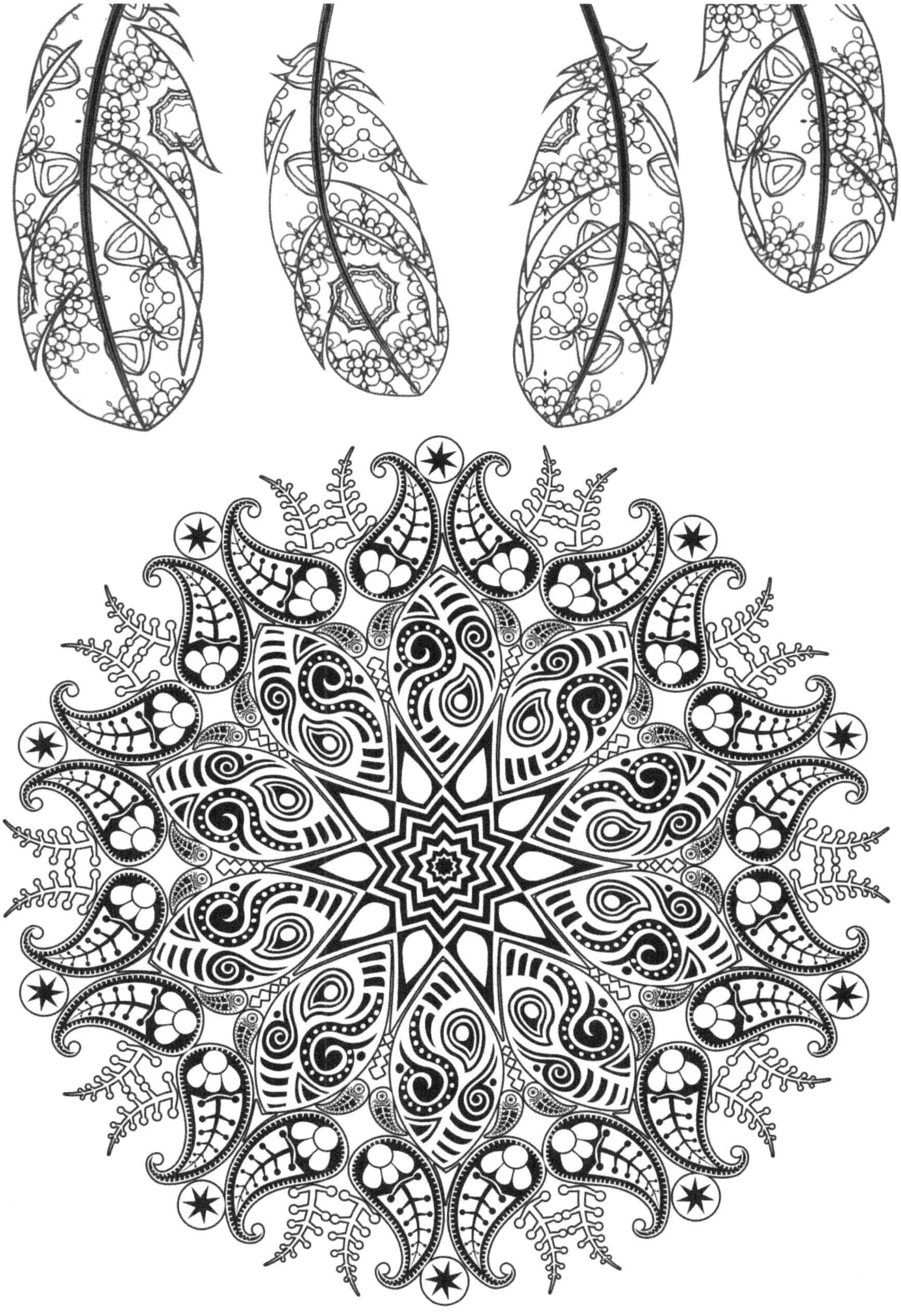

www.ingramcontent.com/pod-product-compliance
Lightning Source LLC
Chambersburg PA
CBHW081751280526
45789CB00008B/2815
* 9 7 8 1 5 3 7 4 3 4 1 8 6 *